Stitch/Style
Sweet Dreams

Stitch/Style
Sweet Dreams

FABULOUS FABRIC SEWING PROJECTS & IDEAS

MARGARET ROWAN

D&C
David and Charles

www.stitchcraftcreate.co.uk

CONTENTS

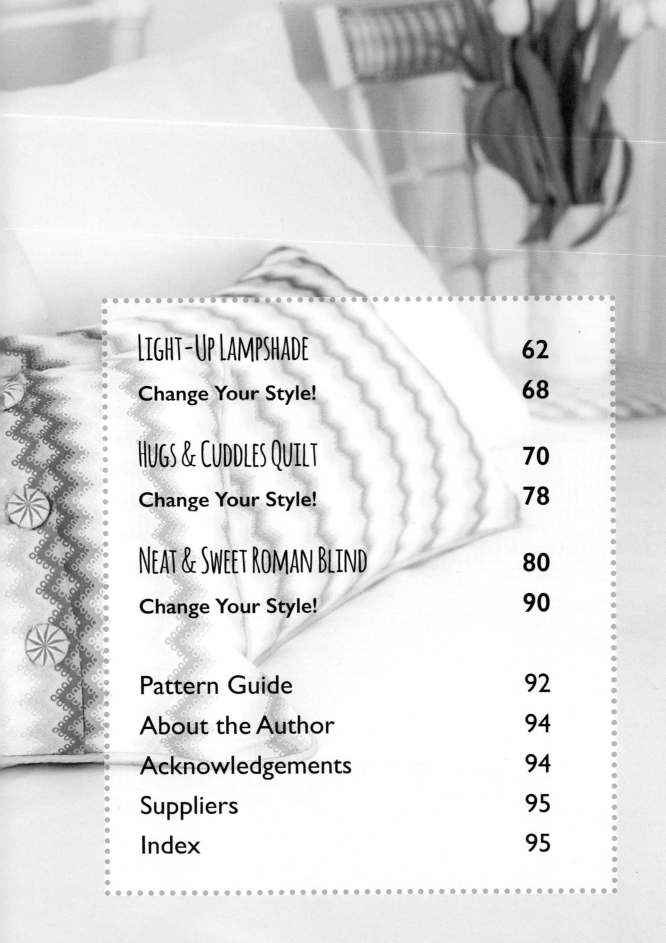

INTRODUCTION

Welcome to *Sweet Dreams*, where you will find stunningly gorgeous fabrics by Tula Pink and Tim Holtz. Every new collection they produce brings another cornucopia of inspiring designs to use to decorate your home.

Tula Pink now delights us with her lovely Foxfield Collection, which hides all sorts of surprises amongst the flora. Take a close look Foxtrot, used to make the Sweet Dreams Duvet Set: at first glance you see a wonderful balance of flowers and leaves, but take a closer look – is that a rabbit? And over there, a shy fox? You will never tire of looking at Tula's fabrics.

Change Your Style!

Check out the Change Your Style! pages of the book to see how you can create a completely different look and feel with the same project but using an alternative material. Tim Holtz's Eclectic Elements fabric collection provides a fantastic mix of timeless tonal hues and typography, together with collections of clock faces, labels and other nostalgic ephemera. Now you can read in bed without getting covered in newsprint!

Sweet Dreams is all about comfort and cosiness, and also about creating your own style by making home accessories with your chosen fabrics rather than ready-made shop-bought items.

The projects require a range of different skills, from creating simple patterns to adding finishing touches such as a zipper and covered buttons and ruffles. The snuggly quilt is made from large rectangles of fabric, so it pieces together very quickly. It is easily made in a day and is a great introduction to quilting.

I hope you gain as much enjoyment from making these projects as I did, and that you will have your very own special projects to curl up under, put on display or wear very soon.

Margaret Rowan

Sweet Dreams Duvet Set

SWEET DREAMS DUVET SET

A well-dressed bed is the crowning glory to any beautifully decorated bedroom, and by making your own duvet set you can ensure yours reflects your own personal style.

This project combines Tula Pink's Vintage Stars and Foxtrot fabrics to create a subtle but decorative shabby-chic look and, once you get used to handling large swathes of fabric, it's so simple to make you'll be dressing every bed in the house!

YOU WILL NEED

Makes one double duvet cover, 190 x 198cm (75 x 78in), and two pillow cases, 48 x 70cm (19 x 27½in)

Duvet Cover

- 250cm (98½in) of **Foxtrot** in *Sunrise*
- 420cm (165⅓in) of **Vintage Stars** in *Sunrise*
- 19mm (¾in) buttons x 9
- Coats cotton thread no. 2427

Pillow Cases

- 170cm (67in) **Foxtrot** in *Sunrise*
- Coats cotton thread no. 2427

Other

- Sewing machine buttonhole attachment.

Preparation time

1½ hours

Sewing time

4 hours

Foxtrot

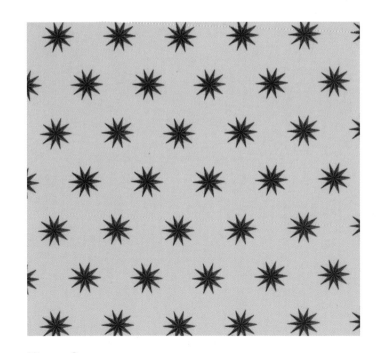

Vintage Stars

PREPARING YOUR FABRIC

Cutting the fabric

There is a 1.5cm (⅝in) seam allowance included on
the pattern

Duvet Cover

- For the Front and Back Panel, cut two full width lengths of 120cm (47in) from Foxtrot.

- For the Front and Back Border, cut four 43 x 200cm (17 x 78¾in) strips from Vintage Stars, cutting the ends at 45 degrees (to mitre).

- Cut four 43 x 214cm (17 x 84¼in) strips from Vintage Stars, cutting the ends at 45 degrees (to mitre).

- For the Button Band, cut two 165 x 7cm (65 x 2¾in) strips from Vintage Stars.

Pillow Cases

- Cut two 51 x 167cm (20 x 65¾in) from Foxtrot.

MAKING THE DUVET SET

Duvet Cover

1. Place a dot on the wrong side (WS) at each corner of the centre panel, 1½cm (⅝in) from each edge. Pin the borders to the centre panel, right sides (RS) facing and within the dots. Stitch in place and press the seams towards the border (Fig. 1).

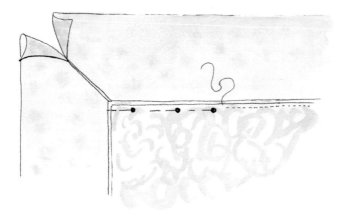

Fig. 1

2. At the corners, pin the mitred seams together, stitch and press open. Repeat for the other half of the duvet. Pin and stitch the sides and top edges of the duvet cover (Fig. 2).

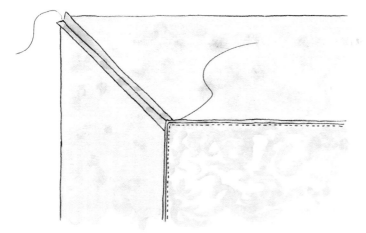

Fig. 2

Attaching the button band

3. Pin each of the button bands centrally to each of the lower edges, RS together, 1½cm (⅝in) in from the short end, to within 1½cm (⅝in) from the far end. Stitch in place (Fig. 3).

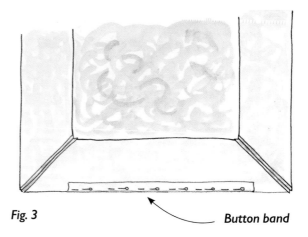

Fig. 3   **Button band**

4. Turn under a 5mm (¼in) hem on the long, raw edges of the button bands. Fold the band in half so that the crease of the hem lies on top of the seam. Fold in the raw edges on the short ends. Pin and edge stitch from the RS.

5. Pin and sew the short section of the seam, either side of the button band (Fig. 4). When you get to the button band, leave the needle down, raise the presser foot and turn the work to continue onto the side of the button band. Zigzag the raw edges on the other three sides.

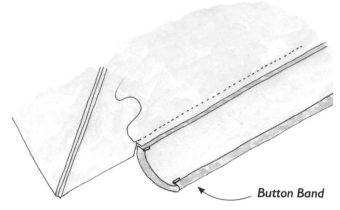

Button Band

Fig. 4

6. Mark the position of nine buttonholes on the button band, approximately 16cm (6¼in) apart and stitch using your buttonhole attachment. Carefully cut the buttonholes.

7. Mark the position of the buttons at the centre of each buttonhole and stitch in place (Fig. 5).

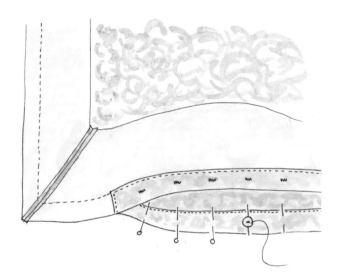

Fig. 5

Pillow Case

8. Take one pillow case piece and turn under a 5mm (¼in) double hem on one short end, edge stitching in place (Fig. 6). (Do this on the reverse end on the second pillow case).

Fig. 6

9. Fold the opposite end over by 10cm (4in), WS together, and then fold under the raw edge by 5cm (2in). Edge stitch (Fig. 7).

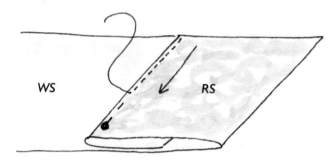

WS   RS

Fig. 7

10. Fold the pillow case, RS facing, so that the wider hem is 70cm (27½in) from the fold. Fold the remaining 14cm (5½in) over the top (Fig. 8).

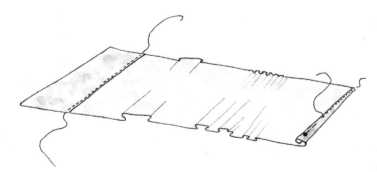

Fig. 8

11. Pin along each side and stitch (Fig. 9). To finish, neaten the raw edges with zigzag stitch, turn through and press. Repeat for the second pillow case.

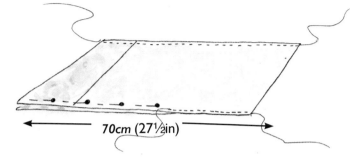

70cm (27½in)

Fig. 9

TIP

When cutting buttonholes, place a pin across each short end, just inside the stitching before cutting with a stitch ripper.

CHANGE YOUR STYLE!

Reading the papers in bed, 'naughty-naughty' but very nice too! Tim's fabric looks so calm here, perfect for a good night's sleep. The letterpress border weighs down the edge of the duvet cover perfectly and gives it a 'news-worthy' finish! Use these fabrics to create a relaxed sophistication that you won't want to wait to enjoy.

Change Your Style using Tim Holtz Eclectic Elements, Dictionary in Neutral and Stamps in Blue.

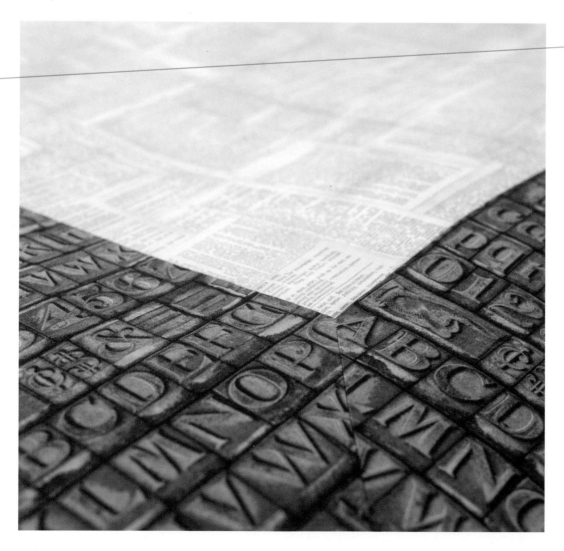

PRETTY BED PILLOWS

Pretty Bed Pillows

Pillows can be used in a bedroom to pull colours and patterns together, add interest and make the room feel cosy and luxurious.

There's nothing more inviting than a pile of pillows on the bed for snoozing and snuggling. Make these smart pillows with button detailing in a contrasting or co-ordinating fabric to add a touch of style.

The covered buttons and piping details give these elegant pillows a really professional finish. Make one or two as statement pieces or a whole pile for a chair or bed.

YOU WILL NEED

Makes one pillow 50 x 30cm (20 x 12in)

- 60cm (23½in) of **Pointed Lace** in *Shade*
- 50cm (20in) of **Vintage Stars** in *Shade*
- 175cm (69in) x 3mm (⅛in) piping cord
- 22mm (¾in) self-covered buttons x 3
- Coats cotton thread, no.2726 and 1310

Preparation time

1 hour

Sewing time

3 hours

TIP

Remember to cut the ends of the bias strips in the same direction otherwise they will not join correctly.

Pointed Lace

Vintage Stars

PREPARING YOUR FABRIC

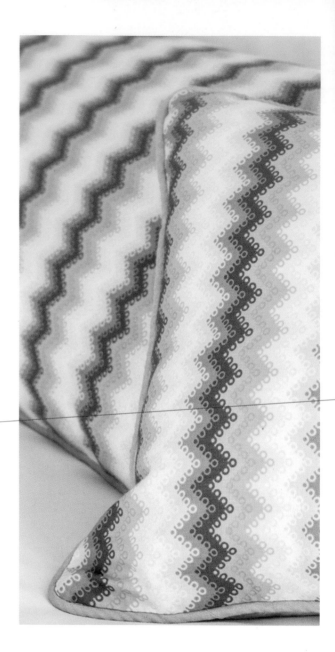

Making the pattern

There is a 1.5cm (⅝in) seam allowance included on
the pattern.

- For the front panel, draw a rectangle 53 x 33cm
  (21 x 13in).

- For the large back panel, draw a rectangle 45 x 33cm
  (17¾ x 13in).

- For the small back panel, draw a rectangle 23 x 33cm
  (9 x 13in).

Cutting the fabric

- Cut one piece of Pointed Lace from each pattern, laying
  the pattern sideways on the fabric so that the zigzag
  runs vertically on the width of the pilow.

- Cut three 4cm (1½in) wide strips of Vintage Stars
  (the design is not on the bias, so cut through the stars)
  for piping.

- Cut three circles of Vintage Stars 3.5cm (1⅓in)
  diameter to cover your buttons.

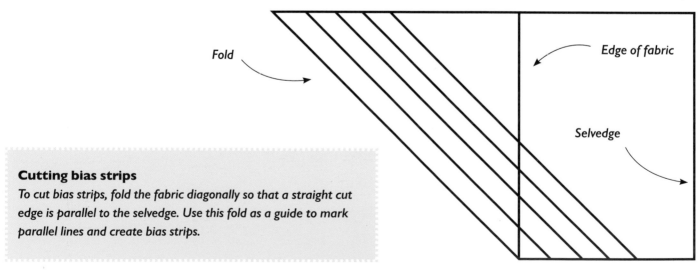

Cutting bias strips
*To cut bias strips, fold the fabric diagonally so that a straight cut
edge is parallel to the selvedge. Use this fold as a guide to mark
parallel lines and create bias strips.*

MAKING THE PILLOW

Piping

1. Begin by joining the bias strips. Trim the ends of each strip to a 45 degree angle (Fig. 1), (when the strips are facing the same way up the ends must lie in the same direction).

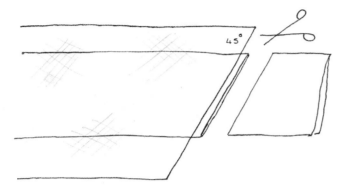

Fig. 1

2. Place the strips right sides (RS) together, so that the short ends overlap to form a 'V' at each side of the seam. Use a small stitch length to join the strips from one side to the other (Fig. 2). Trim the seams to 5mm (¼in) and finger press open.

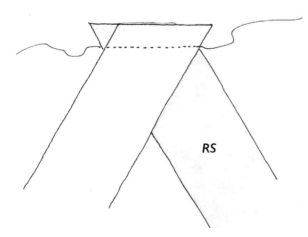

Fig. 2

3. Lay the strips, wrong sides (WS) facing upwards and place the piping cord on top. Fold over the fabric and pin in place. Using an adjustable zipper foot, sew close but not tight to the piping cord. When you get to the end, cut the piping cord (Fig. 3).

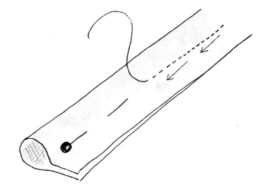

Fig. 3

4. Place the front panel RS facing. Place the end of the piping 5cm (2in) from the top left-hand corner and pin in position. Continue to pin the piping in place, at the corners, snip into the seam allowance of the bias strip to allow it to turn the corner freely (Fig. 4).

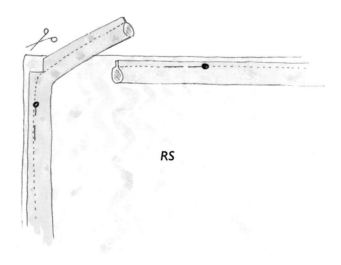

Fig. 4

5. When you get back to the beginning, cut the covered piping cord so that it overlaps the other end by 2cm (¾in). You want there to be a 2cm (¾in) overlap of fabric, but for the piping cord to meet and not overlap – trim the cord accordingly. Remove the stitching at the end of the fabric so that you can turn under the fabric by 1cm (½in) and wrap this around the other end of the covered piping (Fig. 5).

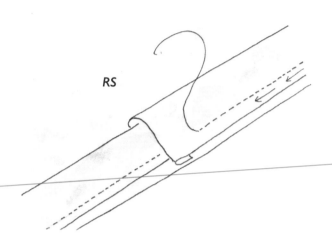

Fig. 5

6. Begin stitching 5cm (2in) from the end of the cord, stitching close to the piping cord but not tight to it. At each corner, lower your machine needle and raise the presser foot to turn your work.

Preparing the backs

7. On the right-hand side of the larger back section turn under a 5mm (¼in) hem and stitch.

8. On the left-hand side of the smaller back section, turn under 1cm (½in) and then turn the raw edge under to the crease. Edge stitch in place (Fig. 6).

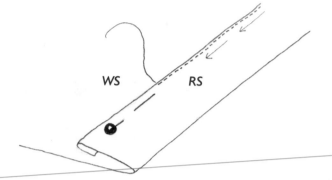

Fig. 6

Joining the front and backs

9. With the front section RS facing upwards, place the larger back section RS down onto the left side. Fold back the right-hand side by 7cm (2¾in). Pin all the way around the three edges.

10. Place the smaller back section RS down onto the right side of the front section. The hemmed edges should lie on top of each other. Pin all the way around and stitch as close as you can to the piping cord. Trim the corners and neaten the raw edges by overlocking or using a zigzag stitch. Turn through and press.

Covering the buttons

11. Cut a circle 8mm (⅜in) larger than the button from Vintage Stars fabric. Place the button on top of the fabric and catch it under the teeth of the button. When there are no creases around the edge, position the back of the button and press hard.

12. Mark the position of the three buttonholes, 2cm (¾in) from the fold. Position the centre buttonhole first, then the other two either side, 4.5cm (1¾in) away from the central one. Stitch using the buttonhole setting on your machine. (You may need to look at your manual if you are not familiar with this process.)

Sewing on the buttons

13. Mark the position of the buttons through the middle of each buttonhole. Bring the needle with a knotted thread through from the back of the cover at the mark and through one of the shanks on the button. Put the needle back into the fabric. Repeat a further six times and fasten off the thread at the back of the cover through the seven small stitches at the back of the button.

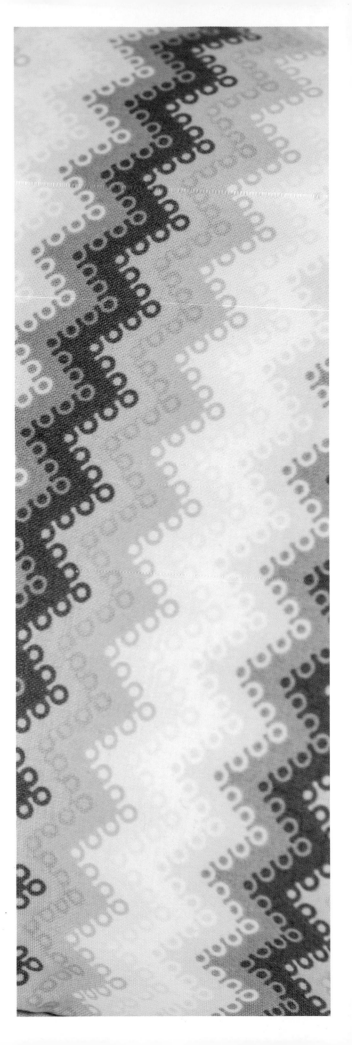

CHANGE YOUR STYLE!

Rectangular pillows are a great shape as they sit perfectly on a chair, providing support without getting in the way! Self-covered buttons create enough interest without detracting too much from this stunning fabric again on a typographical theme—but you can't have too much of good thing! Combine them with the Sweet Dreams Duvet Set for a truly cohesive look.

Change Your Style using Tim Holtz Eclectic Elements, Subway in Taupe and Measurements in Taupe.

Gather-All Laundry Bag

GATHER-ALL LAUNDRY BAG

Bide your time in the run-up to wash day with this great looking laundry bag - the difference between an untidy mountain of laundry and a discreet and practical solution to keeping dirty clothes out of sight.

Stitch strips of patterned fabrics together in stylish patchwork to create an elegant bag, perfect for bedroom, bathroom or laundry room.

YOU WILL NEED

Makes one laundry bag, 55 x 80cm (21½ x 31½in)

- 120cm (47¼in) of **Vintage Stars** in *Dusk*
- 50cm (20in) of **Pony Play** in *Dusk*
- 30cm (12in) of **Baby Geo** in *Dusk*
- 30cm (12in) of **Scribbles** in *Dusk*
- 350cm (137¼in) of 5mm cord
- Coats cotton thread no. 5013
- Interfacing, small offcut
- Sewing machine buttonhole attachment

Preparation time

1 hour

Sewing time

3 hours

TIP

Think about pattern placement when buying your fabric. You may need to buy a little extra to get the right look for your finished project.

Vintage Stars

Pony Play

PREPARING YOUR FABRIC

Baby Geo

Cutting out

There is a 1½cm (⅝in) seam allowance included on the pattern.

- Cut one 94 x 55cm (37 x 21½in) strip across the width from Vintage Stars (this will be the lining and top strip combined).

- Cut one 9 x 55cm (3½ x 21½in) strip across the width from Vintage Stars.

- Cut one 8 x 55cm (3¼ x 21½in) strip across the width from Vintage Stars.

- Cut one 19 x 55cm (7½ x 21½in) strip across the width from Baby Geo.

- Cut one 18 x 55cm (7 x 21½in) strip across the width from Pony Play.

- Cut one 12 x 55cm (4½ x 21½in) strip across the width from Pony Play.

- Cut one 9 x 55cm (3½ x 21½in) strip across the width from Baby Geo.

- Cut one 12cm x 55cm (4½ x 21½in) strip across the width from Scribbles.

- Cut one 7 x 55cm (2¾ x 21½in) strip across the width from Scribbles.

Strap

- Cut one 10cm x 25cm (4 x 10in) piece from Scribbles.

- Cut one 5 x 10cm (2 x 4in) piece of fusible woven interfacing, cut into two 5cm (2in) squares.

Scribbles

MAKING THE BAG

Joining the strips and lining

1. Join the strips in the following order, from the top: 7cm (2¾in) Scribbles, 19cm (7½in) Baby Goo, 8cm (3¼in) Vintage Stars, 18cm (7in) Pony Play, 12cm (4½in) Scribbles, 9cm (3½in) Baby Geo, 12cm (4½in) Pony Play, 9cm (3½in) Vintage Stars, 94cm (37in) lining and top strip (combined) in Vintage Stars.

2. Place each pair of strips right side (RS) facing and pin and stitch the seam. When you get to the Pony Play strips make sure you have them the right way up (Fig. 1).

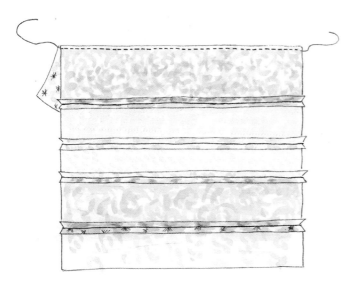

Fig. 1

3. Stitch the large lining to the top strip and then fold in half, it doesn't matter if it's wrong side (WS) or RS at this stage, so that the lower edges of the lining and strips are matching. Trim the sides level if required.

4. On the top strip of Vintage Stars, measure in 28.5cm (11in) from each side and place a pin. Fuse a piece of interfacing on the reverse side where you have placed the pin. Stitch a vertical 2.5cm (1in) buttonhole, 4cm (1½in) above the Scribbles border, on the RS at each pin mark (Fig. 2A).

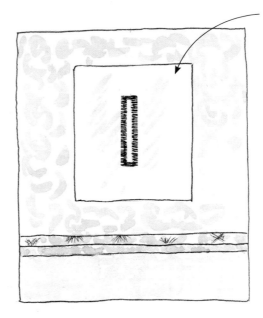

Interfacing

Fig. 2 Wrong side

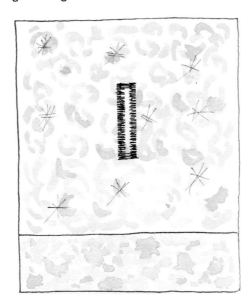

Fig. 2A Right side

5. With RS facing, fold the bag in half vertically, match the strips and pin through the seams (Fig. 3). Stitch and press open the seam. Fold, with RS facing, so that the seam lies centrally down the back of the bag. Pin and stitch across the lower edge of the bottom strip.

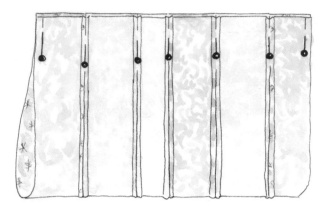

Fig. 3

6. Pin and stitch the lower edge of the lining, leaving a 10cm (4in) gap so that the bag can be turned through. Turn through and press. Pin around the top, either side of the two button holes, back and front. Work two rows of stitching, 4cm (1½in) from the top edge and 4cm (1½in) from the Scribbles border (Fig. 4).

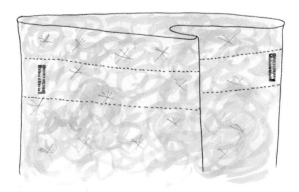

Fig. 4

Strap and cord

7. Take the rectangle of Scribbles and fold in half lengthways, RS facing. Leaving a 5cm (2in) gap on the long side of the strip, begin stitching at the fold on one of the short sides, turning the corner by lowering the needle and raising the presser foot. Continue to the opening, reverse stitch to fasten the thread and begin again at the other side of the of the opening, continuing to stitch the other side. Turn through and press the short edge.

8. Slip stitch the opening. Place on the Scribbles strip, across the centre back seam of the bag. To attach the strap, stitch a small rectangle on each end to secure to the bag (Fig. 5). Thread two lengths of 5mm (¼in) cord through the opening, one from each buttonhole, and knot. To finish, fringe the ends.

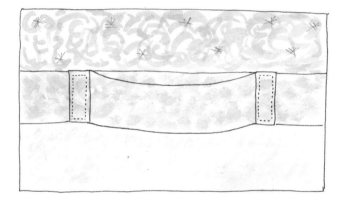

Fig. 5

CHANGE YOUR STYLE!

Moving away from fancy florals, these more masculine-look fabrics are ideal for a teenage boy's bedroom and will bring some order to a world of chaos! Try leaving the top open hanging on the door or as it is here, under a shelf, and maybe they can throw their laundry in from the bed!

Change Your Style using Tim Holtz Eclectic Elements, Ticking in Black, Measurements in Taupe, Game Pieces in Taupe and Travel in Taupe.

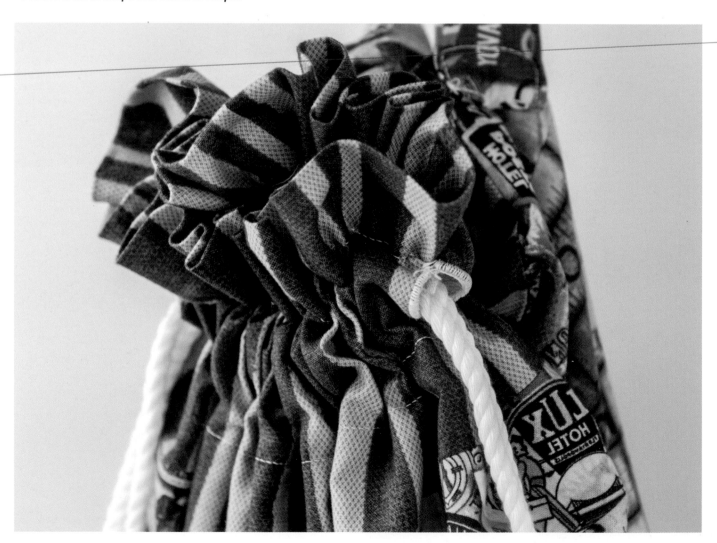

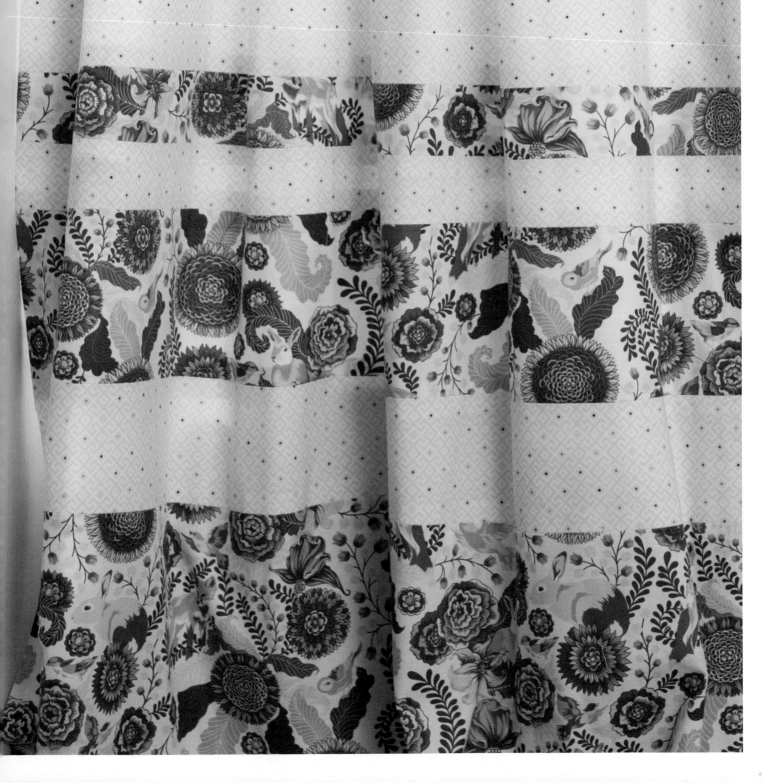

Pretty Pleated Curtains

PRETTY PLEATED CURTAINS

New curtains are a fabulous way of giving any room an entirely different look without the mess and bother of re-painting. The great thing about making your own is that you can match them to all your other soft furnishings for a truly cohesive look. Got fabric left over? Why not make a co-ordinating scatter pillow like the Pretty Bed Pillow? Perfect!

YOU WILL NEED

Makes one pair of curtains, each measuring 100 x 150cm (39⅓ x 59in)

- 280cm (110¼in) of **Baby Geo** in *Sunrise*
- 150cm (39⅓in) of **Foxtrot** in *Sunrise*
- 340cm (134in) of curtain lining
- Lead weights x 4
- 240cm (94½) of 10cm (4in) Fusible Buckram
- Coats cotton thread no. 1418
- Pin hooks x 14

Preparation time

1 hour

Sewing time

4 hours

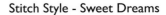

TIP

Add some self-covered buttons at the base of each pleat for a pretty finishing touch.

Baby Geo

Foxtrot

PREPARING YOUR FABRIC

Cutting out

There is a 1.5cm (⅝in) seam allowance included on the pattern. Cut all pieces across the width of the fabric.

From **Baby Geo**:

- A: Cut two pieces measuring 115cm (45¼in) .

- B: Cut two pieces measuring 8cm (3¼in).

- C: Cut two pieces measuring 12cm (4½in).

From **Foxtrot**:

(Remember to match the pattern on both sides of the curtain and check that the design is the right way up.)

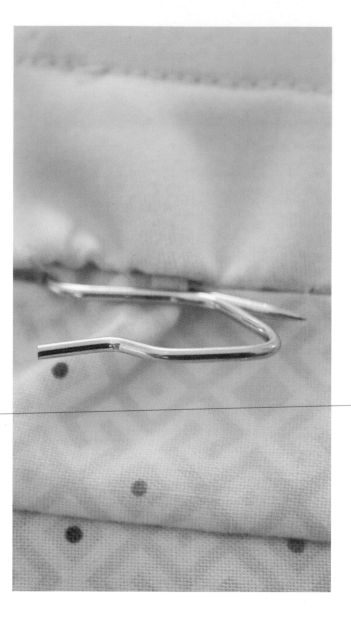

- D: Cut two pieces measuring 38cm (15in).

- E: Cut two pieces measuring 15cm (6in).

- F: Cut two pieces measuring 8cm (3¼in).

From **lining** cut two 160cm (63in) lengths, removing the selvedge from one side only.

From **fusible buckram** cut two 114cm (45in) lengths.

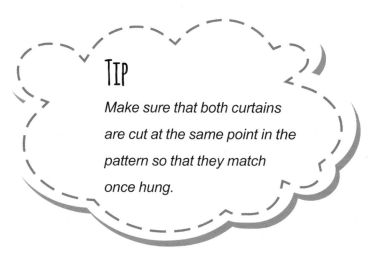

TIP

Make sure that both curtains are cut at the same point in the pattern so that they match once hung.

MAKING THE CURTAIN

1. With right sides (RS) facing, attach section F to the lower edge of section A. Attach section B to section F. Attach section E to section C. Attach section C to section D (Fig. 1). Press all seams open and trim the selvedge off both sides. The width should measure 110cm (43⅓in).

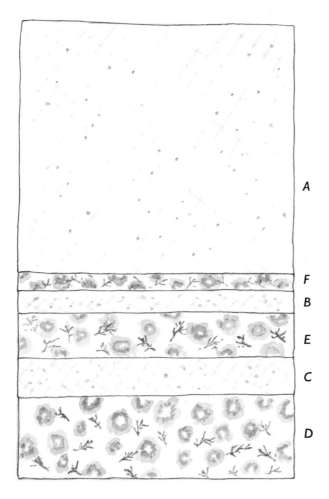

Fig. 1

2. Lay RS down on the corner of a table (this will help you to make the curtain square), aligning the edges of the fabric with the edges of the table. Fold the side turnings in by 5cm (2in) and fold the hem up by 10cm (4in) (Fig. 2). Fold the raw edge of the hem into the crease line to create a double hem.

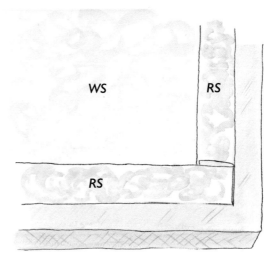

Fig. 2

3. At the corner where the folds meet, stick a pin as shown in Fig. 3. This is called the 'point of mitre'. Keep this pin in place until the mitres are stitched.

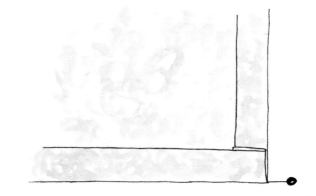

Fig. 3

4. Unfold the hem and fold the corner at a 45 degree angle pivoting from the pin. Crease and carefully refold the side turning and the double hem, you will have a perfectly mitred corner (Fig. 4). Repeat on the other corner.

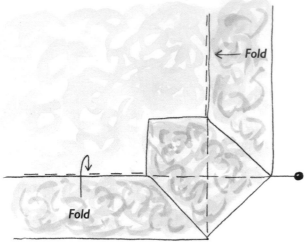

Fig. 4

6. Measure up 150cm (59in) from the hemline and mark the top of the curtain with pins across the width. Fold over and insert the buckram at this point, fusible side facing the WS of the curtain. Fold the sides in and crease, trimming away excess buckram from the side turnings (Fig. 6).

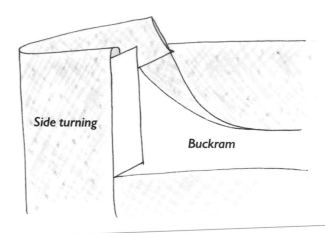

Fig. 6

5. Take a spare piece of lining or scrap fabric, 10 x 40cm (4 x 16in). Fold it in half lengthways, stitch down one side to make a tube and cut into four equal pieces. Place a lead weight in each section, fold in half and stitch across the top. Stitch one in the hem at each corner of the curtain (Fig. 5).

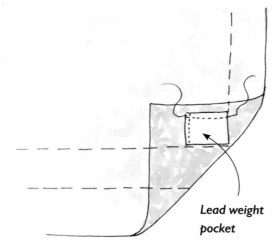

Lead weight pocket

Fig. 5

7. Cut a small wedge-shaped piece off from the top of the turning, on both sides of the buckram (Fig. 7).

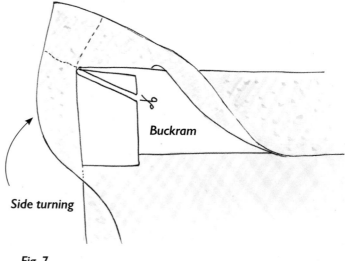

Side turning

Buckram

Fig. 7

8. Fold over the top edge of the curtain and fuse in place with a hot iron. When you get to the side turnings, pull the fabric down over the wedge shape and pleat the fabric inside the turning to remove the extra fabric. The top of the curtain now has a mock mitred effect.

9. With cotton, herringbone stitch the side turnings, from 15cm (6in) from the top left hand side to the mitred corner at the lower edge, making your stitches about 4cm (1½in) apart. When you get to the corner, use a small ladder stitch to join the two folds of the mitre together. Work down to the corner and back up to the top of the hem (Fig. 8). Continue along the hem using a smaller herringbone stitch then work the second mitre and the right hand turning, stopping 15cm (6in) from the top.

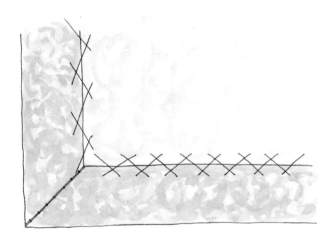

Fig. 8

Lining

10. Take a piece of lining fabric and with the WS facing, fold up the hem by 5cm (2in), then fold the raw edge into the crease and press to create a 2.5cm (1in) double hem. Edge stitch in place (Fig. 9) before repeating with the second lining.

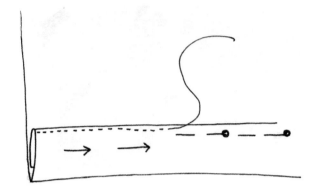

Fig. 9

11. Place the top edge of the lining hem to the top edge of the curtain hem (Fig. 10). The trimmed edge of the lining is placed to the edge of the curtain.

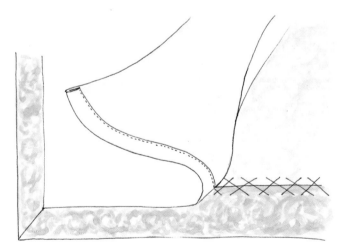

Fig. 10

45

12. Fold under the side, turning so that the raw edge of the lining meets the edge of the curtain. Crease and pin in position. The corner of the lining should now sit on the mitre (Fig. 11).

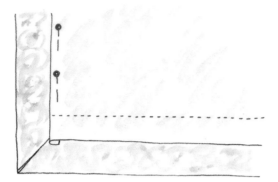

Fig. 11

13. On the other side, fold the lining back to the edge of the curtain and trim the excess away. Fold under the side, turning so that the raw edge of the lining meets the edge of the curtain. Crease and pin in position.

14. Fold back the lining from top to bottom and stitch using a locking in stitch – make a small stitch on the lining then a small stitch of a couple of threads on the back of the curtain. Make the next stitch 15cm (6in) away. Loop the thread downwards and make another stitch on the lining and one on the curtain. The stitch will be 'locked', similar to a large buttonhole or blanket stitch (Fig. 12). Repeat on the other side of the curtain.

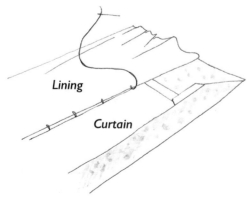

Fig. 12

15. Turn under the top of the curtain lining so that it sits 5mm (¼in) from the top edge of the curtain (Fig. 13).

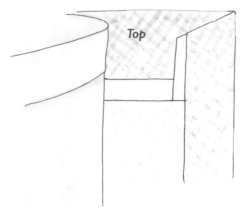

Fig. 13

16. Begin sewing 4cm (1½in) from the corner of the left-hand side of the hem. Use ladder stitch to the corner, and then up the side to the top corner. Do not stitch through to the front of the curtain. Along the top edge use a prick stitch to hold the lining in place.

17. Ladder stitch down the right-hand side and along 4cm (1½in) of the hem.

Pleats

18. Mark the position of the pleats along the top of the curtain with pins. From the edge, measure and mark 5cm (2in), then mark at every 10cm (4in), ending 5cm (2in) from the opposite edge. To form the first pleat, fold the top of the curtain between the first and second pins, with RS facing. Pin 5cm (2in) from the fold.

19. Repeat with the next and consecutive pairs of pins. Stitch the pleats in place from the top of the curtain to the bottom of the buckram. To hang the curtains, place a pin hook on either side, on the reverse of the curtain at the edge of the lining, so that the hook reaches the top of the lining. Then place one beside each line of stitching on the pleat. Repeat the whole process to create the second curtain, remembering to match the fold of the hems on the Foxtrot design.

Change Your Style!

Eclectic Curtains, what can I say! The contrast between the clock faces and the collection of receipts on the main part of the fabric is fantastic. You can alter the dimensions to suit your own windows – you just need to know the length and width measurements of your window. If you made each curtain to fit the width of the window you would have plenty of fabric to pleat into this pretty pair. To alter the length of the curtains, make the length adjustment to the top section of the curtain, not the bottom.

Change Your Style using Tim Holtz Eclectic Elements, Document in Taupe and Time Piece in Neutral.

SNUGGLY PYJAMA BOTTOMS

SNUGGLY PYJAMA BOTTOMS

There's nothing more relaxing than lounging about in easy-to-wear pyjama bottoms, whether it's for a long, leisurely weekend breakfast or a late night movie curled up on the sofa.

The elasticated waist keeps the fit comfortable whatever you're doing. The handy pockets make these pyjama bottoms practical, and the binding and tie belt give them an informal elegance.

YOU WILL NEED

Makes size 12 pyjama bottoms. Finished length 100cm (40in), hip 118cm (46½in).

- 240cm (94½in) of **Serpentine** in *Dusk*
- 50cm (20in) of **Foxtrot** in *Dusk*
- Coats cotton thread no. 9141 x 2
- 45 x 2.5cm (17¾ x 1in) soft elastic

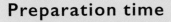

Preparation time

2 hours

Sewing time

4 hours

Serpentine

Foxtrot

TIP

Make sure that the pattern matches around each leg by placing the hem at the same point of the design.

PREPARING YOUR FABRIC

Drawing the pattern

For the back, front and tie belt patterns, go to Pattern Guide. There is a 1.5cm (⅝in) seam allowance included in the pattern.

Waistband

- For the back waistband and facing, cut one rectangle 7 x 31.5cm (2¾ x 12½in). Mark one short end to place to a fold.

- For the front waistband, cut one rectangle 7 x 24.5cm (2¾ x 9¾in).

- For the front waistband, cut one rectangle 7 x 4cm (2¾ x 1½in). Mark one short end to place to a fold.

- For the front waistband facing, cut one rectangle 7 x 25.5cm (2¾ x 10¼in).

Pockets

- For the pocket back, referring to the pattern, trace off the large curve and the complete corner of the front trousers.

- For the pocket facing, referring to the pattern, trace off the smaller curve and the large curve, join the curves with the short sections of side and waist edges.

- For the pocket frills, cut a rectangle 36 x 6cm (14 x 2½in).

Cutting the fabric

Pre-wash fabric before cutting out:

From Serpentine:

- Cut two fronts and backs.

- Cut one back waistband (place one short end to a fold).

- Cut two large pocket backs.

- Cut two pocket facings.

From Foxtrot:

- Cut one centre front waistband (place one short end to a fold).

- Cut two side front waistbands.

- Cut two pocket frills (cut on the bias).

- Cut two strips, 5 x 56cm (2 x 22in) for the hem binding.

- Cut two tie belt pieces (place one long end to a fold).

MAKING THE PYJAMAS

Back

1. Take the two back pieces and, with right sides (RS) together, pin and stitch the centre back seam. On the right-hand side, trim away half of the seam (this is known as a lapped seam) (Fig. 1). Fold the left-hand side of the seam to the right and fold under the trimmed half. Pin and edge stitch in place (Fig. 2).

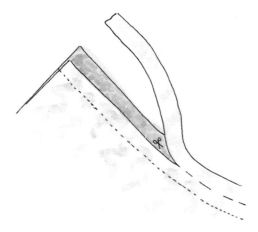

Fig. 1

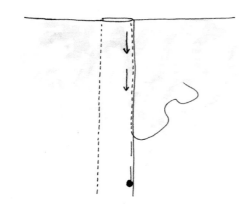

Fig. 2

Front

2. Take the two back pieces and, with RS together, pin and stitch the centre front seam. On the right-hand side, trim away half of the seam. Fold the left-hand side to the right and fold under the trimmed half. Pin and edge stitch in place.

Pocket Frills

3. Fold the pocket frills in half lengthwise, wrong sides (WS) facing, and (with a long stitch and loosened tension) sew two rows of stitching 6mm (¼in) apart within the seam allowance (Fig. 3). Repeat on the other frill.

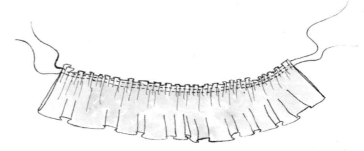

Fig. 3

4. Stay stitch the edges of the pockets (this prevents curved seams from stretching, whilst constructing the garment). Attach the frills to the pockets by matching the raw edges and distributing the gathers evenly along the pocket edge, pinning the frill towards the edge. Stitch in place, 1cm (½in) from the edge (Fig. 4).

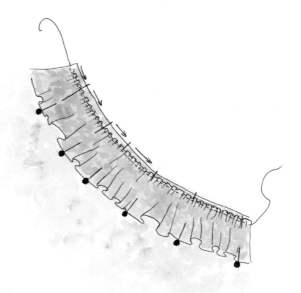

Fig. 4

5. Place the small pocket section, RS facing to the pocket on the front of the pyjamas. Pin and stitch the curved seam. Clip the seam allowance. With the pyjama leg on your left, press the pocket to your right and pin through all thicknesses on the pocket side of the seam and topstitch (Fig. 5).

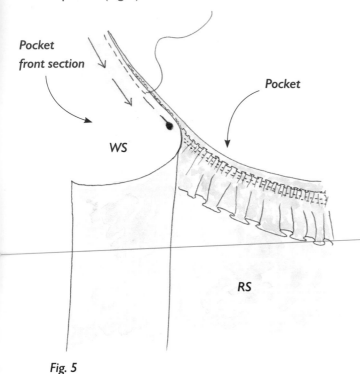

Fig. 5

6. Place the pyjamas down, WS facing, and place the large pocket section RS down so that the edges of the pocket match and the top and sides of the pyjamas match. Pin and stitch around the curved lower edge. Overlock or zigzag to neaten. Repeat on the other pocket. Stitch across the top of the pockets within the seam allowance.

Side seams

7. Place the front and back side seams RS facing. Trim away half of the front part of the seam and fold under the remaining half of the seam. Pin and edge stitch in place. Repeat with the other leg, reversing the direction of the fold.

Inside leg seams

8. Join the front and the back together by matching the seam at the crotch, RS together, pin and stitch the inside leg seam ankle to ankle. Trim away half of the seam on the front half of the seam, folding under the trimmed half, to create a lapped seam as you did in Step 1. Pin and edge stitch in place.

Bound hems

9. Press each strip of binding in half lengthways and then fold the raw edges to the centre crease and press. Place the short ends, RS together, pin and stitch to join the strips together.

10. Pin and stitch the binding to the hem of each leg. Stitch on the first crease. Finger press the seam open. Fold the binding over the edge of the hem and turn under the crease. Pin and either slip stitch in place by hand or machine stitch 'in the ditch' from the RS (Fig. 6).

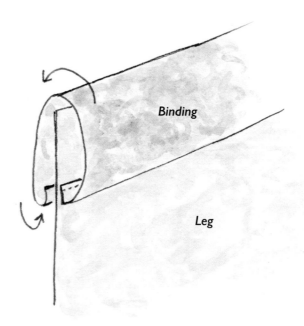

Fig. 6

Waistband and ties

11. Make the ties by folding each piece in half, lengthways, with the RS facing. Pin and stitch around the tie, leaving the narrow end open so that you can turn the tie through. Clip the curved seam, trim the corners (Fig. 7) and finger press the seams open. Turn the tie through using a knitting needle to help – push the pointed end of the tie inside itself and place the blunt end of the knitting needle inside. Pull the tie over the needle (Fig. 8). Make sure your seams are pressed and the corners are pulled out neatly.

Slots for the tie belt

12. Using the three Serpentine sections of waistband, with RS facing, attach the short ends of the centre front waistband section to the side front sections. On each side of the centre panel, sew a 1.5cm (⅝in) seam from the edge towards the middle. Reverse stitch each side of the opening to prevent them from falling apart, leaving an opening to pass the tie through (Fig. 9). Press seams open and turn under the raw edges and top stitch in place.

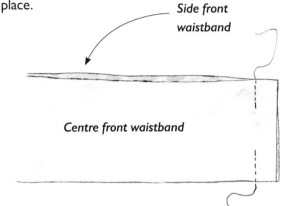

Side front waistband

Centre front waistband

Fig. 9

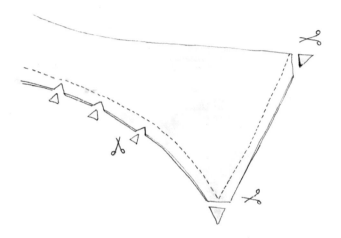

Fig. 7

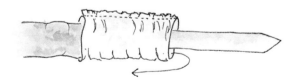

Fig. 8

13. With the two front waistband pieces, place RS facing. Pin and stitch the top seam (Fig. 10). Press open. Repeat with the back waistband pieces. Fold each waistband section in half through the centre front and centre back. Finger press a crease (this will allow you to match the waistband to the centre front and centre back seams).

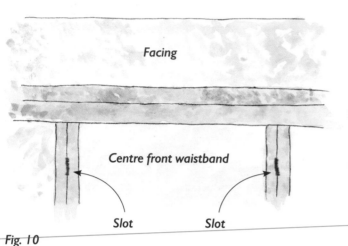

Fig. 10

14. Position the elastic on the back of the facing section of the waistband. Tack (baste) at either end. Place the front and back waistband sections RS facing. Pin and stitch the side seams. Press open the seams (Fig. 11).

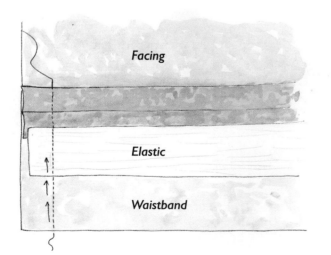

Fig. 11

15. Position the raw edge of the tie centrally under the front side seam allowance, pin and stitch to the seam allowance only. Pull the tie belt through the slots. Fold the waistband in half along the top seam and press. Topstitch 5mm (¼in) from the edge, being sure to avoid catching the tie belt or the elastic (Fig. 12).

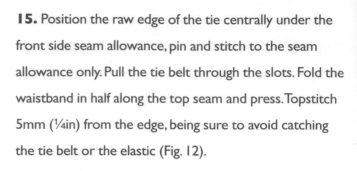

Fig. 12

Attaching the waistband

16. Match the side seams, the centre front and centre back creases to the front and back seams. Pin and stitch in place, avoiding catching the elastic or the tie belts (these can be kept out of the way by folding in half lengthways and pinning on the RS). Press the seam up from the front.

17. Fold under the turning on the facing and either slip stitch or stitch 'in the ditch' from the RS around the lower edge of the waistband. Stretch the back section of the waistband and pin the elastic in place at intervals so that the fabric gathers evenly along the back.

18. To finish, use a long stitch length to sew along the centre of the back section of the waistband to fold the elastic in place.

Change Your Style!

Everyone loves a pair of pyjamas to lounge around or sleep in! This luggage label design would be a great idea for holiday PJs and are masculine enough for boys and men. Why not make matching pairs for the whole family?

Change Your Style using Tim Holtz Eclectic Elements, Travel in Taupe and Ticking in Taupe.

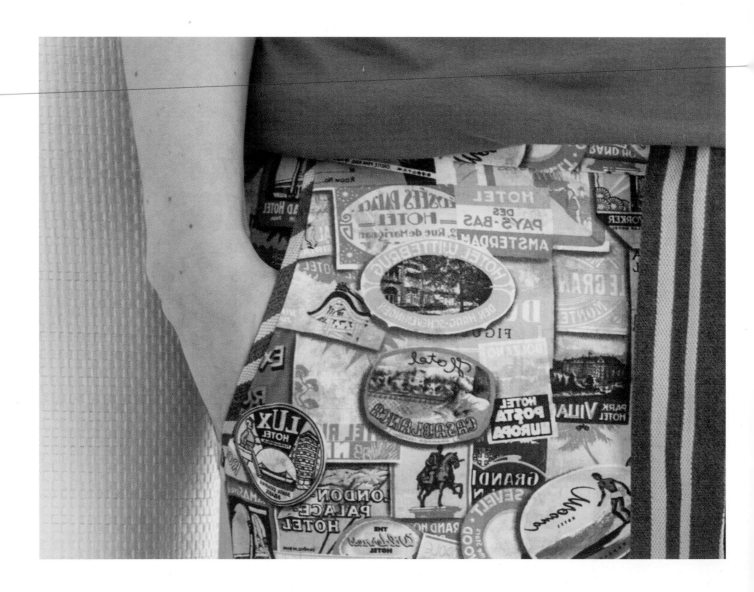

Light-Up Lampshade

LIGHT-UP LAMPSHADE

There's something so sophisticated about fabric lampshades which offer the finishing touch to any room, but who knew they were so easy to make!

With the help of a simple kit and your choice of sumptuous fabric, you could wow all your guests with the fact that you made the fabulous lampshade yourself. Be warned though, once you start, you'll be eyeing every light fitting in sight!

YOU WILL NEED

Each finished lampshade will measure 30cm (12in) high

- 30cm (12in) oval lampshade kit
- 40cm (16in) of **Scribbles** in *Sunshine*
- Sharp scissors or rotary cutter and mat
- Steel ruler or rotary cutting grid
- Double-sided tape

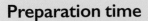

Preparation time

15 minutes

Sewing time

1 hour

TIP

Make sure you have all the tools you need to hand and plenty of uncluttered space.

Scribbles

MAKING THE LAMPSHADE

I. Remembering to think about any pattern placement, cut the fabric to a manageable size, about 4cm (1½in) larger than the self-adhesive lampshade panel.

2. Iron the fabric to remove the creases and any loose fibres and place wrong side (WS) up. Place the lampshade panel on top of the fabric and draw around the lampshade panel (Fig. 1).

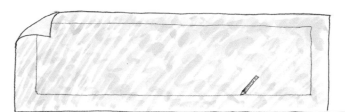

Fig. 1

3. Remove 10cm (4in) of the backing paper and place the panel adhesive side down, within the drawn outline on the fabric. When you are happy that the lampshade panel is in the correct position, pull the paper with your right hand and smooth the lampshade panel onto the fabric with your left hand (Fig. 2). Trim away any excess fabric from the edges of the panel with a sharp blade or rotary cutter.

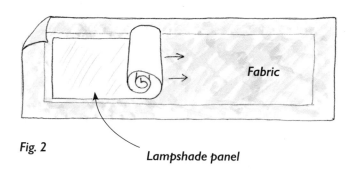

Fabric

Fig. 2

Lampshade panel

4. Snap back the top and bottom edges of the lampshade panel along the scored lines and peel back the adhesive strips (Fig. 3).

Fig. 3

5. Place a strip of double-sided tape along the right-hand edge of the lampshade panel to form the side seam, then stick adhesive tape around both rings of the lampshade kit. Remove the backing strips from the tape and place the rings on either edge of the lampshade panel.

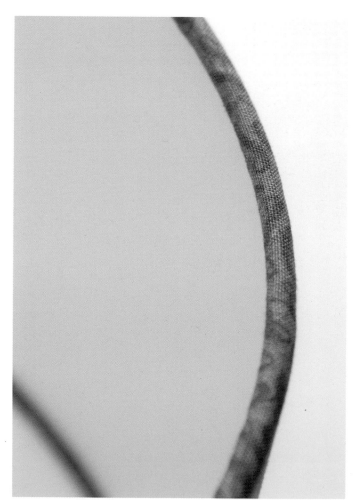

6. Carefully roll the rings around the panel, making sure that they remain in line. Remove the strip on the side edge to close the panel and press firmly to create your seam.

7. Turn the excess fabric around the edges of the lampshade (Fig. 4). Using the serrated tool provided in the kit, carefully push the excess fabric under the ring. Finally, run the smooth side of the tool around the inside of each ring to ensure a smooth finish.

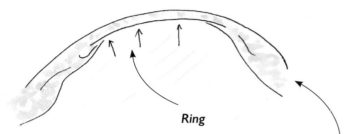

Ring

Fig. 4   *Excess fabric*

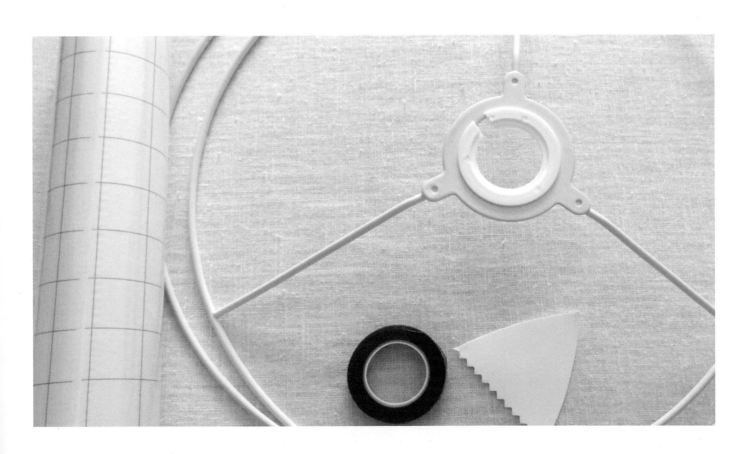

CHANGE YOUR STYLE!

How smart is this! The simplicity of this lampshade-making method means you can create your own lampshades using exactly the fabric that suits your décor. This beautiful Tim Holtz fabric is ideal for a vintage-style study — the perfect handmade gift!

Change Your Style using Tim Holtz Eclectic Elements, Butterflight in Red.

Hugs & Cuddles Quilt

HUGS & CUDDLES QUILT

Whatever the season, there's nothing like snuggling up in a blanket with the family for a movie. Make sure everyone stays cosy with a super-size quilt, hand-stitched with love.

Follow our design to show off a range of beautiful fabrics or get creative and adapt it to suit your own tastes — though we think this one's perfect as it is!

YOU WILL NEED

The finished quilt will measure 175 x 200cm (69 x 78 ¾in)

Blocks

- 30cm (12in) of **Scribbles** in *Dusk*
- 30cm (12in) of **Vintage Stars** in *Dusk*
- 30cm (12in) of **Botanica** in *Dusk*
- 30cm (12in) of **Baby Geo** in *Dusk*
- 30cm (12in) of **Pony Play** in *Dusk*
- 30cm (12in) of **Hoppy Dot** in *Dusk*
- 30cm (12in) of **Baby Geo** in *Shade*

Borders & Blocks

- 250cm (98½ in) of **Pointed Lace** in *Dusk*

Borders, Blocks & Backing

- 480cm (189in) of **Hoppy Dot** in *Shade*
- 200 x 200cm (78¾ x 78¾in-) of quilt wadding (batting) x 2
- Coats cotton thread no. 5013 x 2

Other

- 2.5cm (1in) binding maker

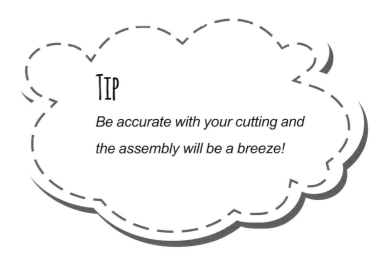

TIP

Be accurate with your cutting and the assembly will be a breeze!

Preparation time

1 hour

Sewing time

6 hours

PREPARING YOUR FABRIC

Cutting out

There is a 6mm (¼in) seam allowance included on the pattern. Cut your pieces in the following order:

Blocks

- Cut two 11.5cm (4¼in) strips across the width of the fabric from Scribbles in Dusk.

- Cut three 11.5cm (4½in) strips across the width of the fabric from Vintage Stars in Dusk.

- Cut two 11.5cm (4½in) strips across the width of the fabric from Botanica in Dusk.

- Cut two 11.5cm (4½in) strips across the width of the fabric from Baby Geo in Dusk.

- Cut two 11.5cm (4½in) strips across the width of the fabric from Pony Play in Dusk.

- Cut three 11.5cm (4½in) strips across the width of the fabric from Hoppy Dot in Dusk.

- Cut three 11.5cm (4½in) strips across the width of the fabric from Baby Geo in Shade.

- Cut three 11.5cm (4½in) strips across the width of the fabric from Pointed Lace in Dusk.

- Cut two 11.5cm (4½in) strips across the width of the fabric from Hoppy Dot in Shade.

- Cut each of the above strips in to 31.75cm (12½in) lengths.

Backing

- Cut the large backing piece of Hoppy Dot in Shade into two. Cut one of them in half down the length.

Borders

- Cut four 7.5cm (3in) strips from the length of Hoppy Dot in Shade.

- Cut four 16.5cm (6½in) strips from the length of Pointed Lace in Dusk.

Binding

- Cut four 5cm (2in) wide strips from the length of Hoppy Dot in Shade.

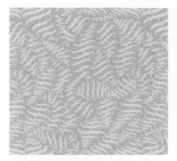

Scribbles, Dusk

Vintage Stars, Dusk

Botanica, Dusk

Baby Geo, Dusk

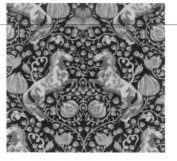

Pony Play, Dusk

Hoppy Dot, Dusk

Pointed Lace, Dusk

Baby Geo, Shade

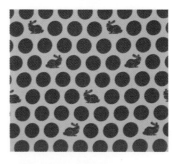

Happy Dot, Shade

MAKING THE QUILT

Blocks

1. Lay out the blocks as in Fig. 1.

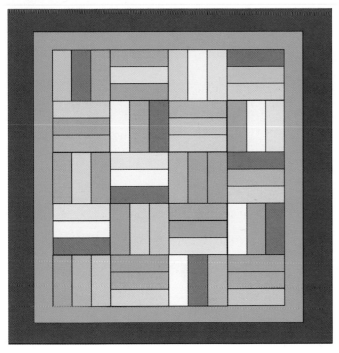

Fig. 1

Key

▨	Scribbles	Dusk
▧	Pointed Lace	Dusk
▨	Vintage Stars	Dusk
▨	Baby Geo	Dusk
▨	Pony Play	Dusk
▨	Botanica	Dusk
▨	Hoppy Dot	Shade
☐	Baby Geo	Shade
▨	Hoppy Dot	Dusk

2. Begin by sewing the three strips for each block together using a 6mm (¼in) seam allowance. Press the seams open (Fig. 2).

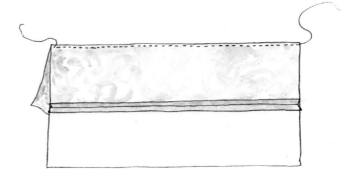

Fig. 2

3. When all the blocks are completed, stitch four blocks together in rows, using Fig. 1 as a guide. Press the seams to the side.

4. When all five rows are completed, attach Row 1 to Row 2. Carefully match the crossed seams between the blocks with a pin through the seam. Press the seams to the side (Fig. 3)

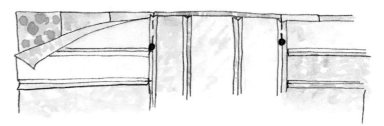

Fig. 3

5. Continue to attach the rows together until you have completed your centre panel. On the reverse of the centre panel, mark a dot 6mm (¼in) from each side at the corner.

6. Attach the centre of each Hoppy Dot strip to each side of the centre panel and pin between the corner dots. Attach the centre of each Pointed Lace border to the centre of each Hoppy Dot border. Pin and stitch.

7. Fold the centre panel diagonally so that the side seams are together. The fold will be at a 45 degree angle. Make sure that the borders are lying flat and the seams are matching.

8. Place a measuring grid over the fold, allowing for a 6mm (¼in) seam allowance on the borders. Trim the border fabrics at this angle using a rotary cutter. Pin the borders, matching the border seam with a pin placed through the seam, and stitch from the corner to the dot at the corners of the centre panel. Note: your stitching line should be on the same line as the fold and your cutting line, 6mm (¼in) from your stitching line.

Backing

9. Place one half length of the Hoppy Dot backing on each side of the whole length. Match the pattern, pin and slip tack (baste) in position. Machine stitch the seams. Trim away excess fabric and press the seam open. Repeat on the other side.

Layering the quilt

10. Place the quilt backing on the table, wrong sides (WS) facing up. Making sure it is lying square to the table and without any creases, tape it onto the table with masking tape. Place the wadding (batting) on top, and tape it down. Now lay the quilt top down, right sides (RS) facing up, and tape down. Tack (baste) all three layers together from the centre out to the edges. Quilt 'in the ditch' between the rows of blocks and around the borders. Trim any excess wadding (batting) and backing to match the quilt top.

11. Join the lengths of binding together and pass through a binding maker, ironing the binding as it emerges. Place the raw edge of the binding to the edge of the quilt and pin and stitch in place. At the corners, mitre the binding. To finish, fold the binding over the raw edges and pin and slip or ladder stitch in place.

CHANGE YOUR STYLE!

Time slips away very quickly under this stunning quilt! How cosy this will be in the autumn and winter – ideal for curling up in front of a movie or for a family duvet day. These super colours would work almost anywhere!

Change Your Style using Tim Holtz Eclectic Elements, Ticking in Red, Subway in Taupe, Games Pieces in Neutral, Measurements in Neutral, French Script in Taupe, Time Pieces in Neutral and Travel in Neutral.

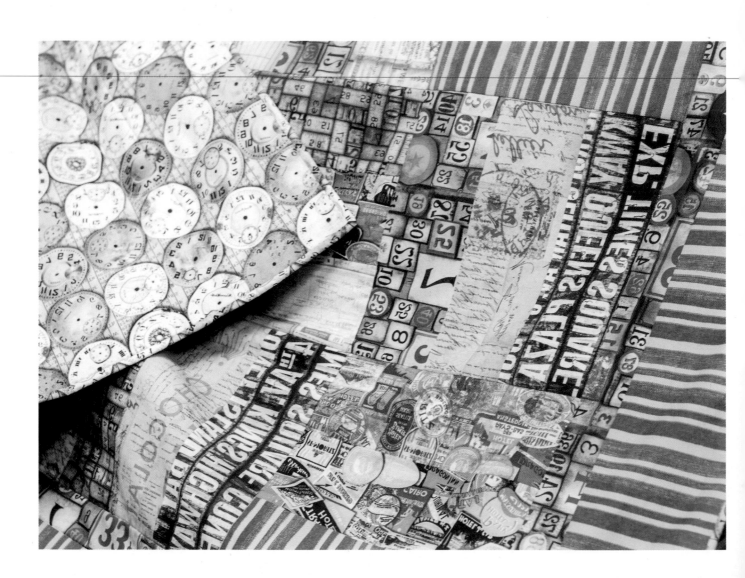

NEAT & SWEET ROMAN BLIND

NEAT & SWEET ROMAN BLIND

Roman blinds are the perfect window dressing when you don't want the bulk of curtains but you still want to preserve privacy and keep out the light

These roman blinds are surprisingly simple to make so why not give this project a go and give a stylish and handmade finish to all your windows.

YOU WILL NEED

The finished blind will measure 120 x 100cm (47¼ x 39⅓in)

- 140cm (55in) of **Serpentino** in *Shade*
- 140cm (55in) of interlining
- 160cm (63in) of lining
- 110cm (43⅓in) fibreglass or steel blind rods x 3
- 120cm (47¼in) of hook and loop fastening
- 110cm (43⅓in) aluminium batten
- Rivets and washers x 12
- 900cm (355in) blind cord
- 2.5 x 5 x 120cm (1 x 2 x 47¼in) wooden batten
- Screw eyes x 5
- Cleat
- Acorn
- Coats cotton sewing thread no. 1310
- Coats extra strong thread, ivory

Tool Kit

- Staple gun
- Saw
- Drill and drill bit
- Prym hole punch riveter
- Bradawl
- Yardstick (optional)

Preparation time

30 minutes

Sewing time

4 hours

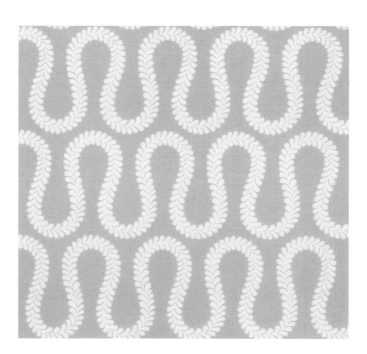

Serpentine

MAKING THE BLIND

Blind

1. Make sure the fabric is cut square across the width by pulling a weft thread (the threads across the width of the fabric). Place the fabric right side (RS) down on the table.

2. Remove the selvedge or cut into it at an angle to release the tension. Align the edges of the fabric with the edge of the table to ensure you are keeping it square. Fold in the sides by 5cm (2in) and finger press.

3. Remove the selvedge from one side of the interlining and place into the crease of one of the side turnings (Fig. 1). Smooth the interlining across to the other side of the blind using a yardstick. or your hands Push into the crease of the fabric and crease the interlining. Remove the excess interlining.

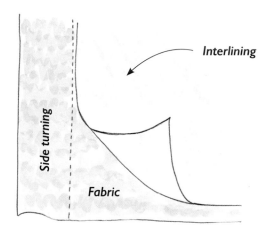

Interlining

Side turning

Fabric

Fig. 1

4. Measure up 10cm (4in) from the lower edge and mark with pins across the width. Fold up the hem on this line and mark the point of each corner with a pin. These pins will remain in place until the blind is nearly finished.

5. From the pins at the hemline, pull the side turnings 2cm (¾in) towards the centre and re-crease, removing the excess interlining (Fig. 2).

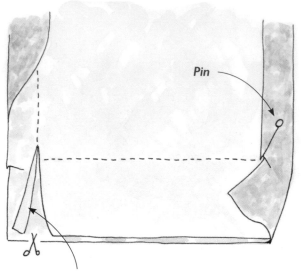

Pin

Excess interlining

Fig. 2

6. Pleat the excess fabric (Fig. 2). Repeat on the other side. Using the strong thread, herringbone each side turning in place (Fig. 3).

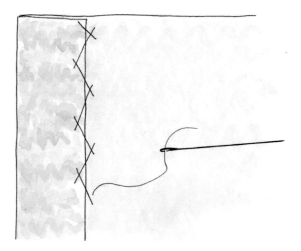

Fig. 3

Lining

7. Remove the selvedge from the lining fabric and place to the side of the blind. Smooth the lining across the blind with a yardstick. Fold the excess lining back on the edge of the blind and remove the excess lining.

8. Turn the sides under by 2.5 cm (1in) so that the raw edges of the lining and blind meet (Fig. 4). Crease the sides of the lining.

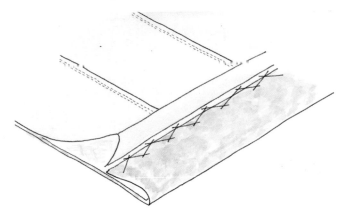

Fig. 4

Marking the position of the rod pockets

9. Place a pin on the side turning next to the lining, 15cm (6in) from the corner pin. Place another two pins at 26cm (10½in) intervals. Repeat on the other side.

10. Place a pin at either side of the lining at 15cm (6in), then another 4cm (1½in) higher. The next two pins are a further 26cm (10½in) and 4cm (1½in). Repeat once more, and repeat on the other side.

11. After double checking that the rod pockets are in the correct position and are completely straight, draw a faint pencil line across the lining between the pins. Fold the rod pockets, WS facing, and pin through on the pencil lines. Reverse stitch at both ends. Stitch another row half-way between the fold and the first stitch line. Repeat with the other rod pockets.

12. Place the lining back down onto the blind and align the rod pockets with the pins, marking their position on the side turnings. Pin the lining in place and ladder stitch the sides (Fig. 5). When you get to each rod pocket, make a couple of extra small stitches to anchor the rod pocket.

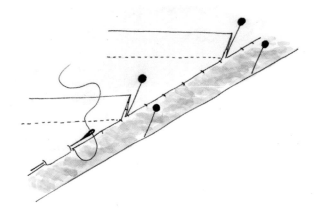

Fig. 5

13. Turn up the hem, turning under the raw edges to the crease. Pin and ladder stitch the right-hand side, then at 5cm (2in) from the edge, stab stitch through the blind to the front and back again, attaching the three layers (Fig. 6). Continue across the hem but do not stitch down the left-hand side, just leave the thread ready to close the seam after inserting the batten.

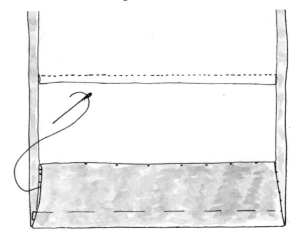

Fig. 6

14. Mark the position of the top of the blind by measuring up 100cm (40in) from the hem. Do this across the width at regular intervals and place a pin at each 100cm (40in) mark. Draw a line across (this will be the finished length) and then draw another one 2cm (¾in) above (this is your cutting line). Cut through all three layers on the second line. Fold back the lining and trim out the interlining at the top of the blind (Fig. 7).

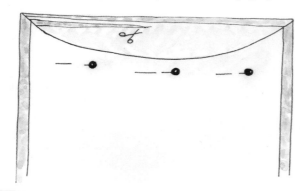

Fig. 7

15. Pin along the top of the blind, 8cm (3¼in) from the top and fold over the top of the blind. You will feel a dip where you cut away the interlining. Position the hook and loop fastening to the top of the blind at this point on the RS and pin in place.

Rod pockets

16. The three layers of the blind have to be stitched together to prevent the blind from sagging. Fasten on the thread at the side of the lining and bring the needle out through the seam of the rod pocket, 2.5 cm (1in) in from the side. Stab stitch through all the layers and bring the needle back through to the lining. Pass the needle behind the lining and bring out 10cm (4in) further along the rod pocket. Make another stab stitch through all of the layers and repeat this along the length of each of the rod pockets.

Hook and loop fastening

17. Machine stitch in place the top of the hook and loop fastening and then stitch the other edge down by hand, stab stitching through at the same points, as on the rod pockets.

Rods and Batten

18. Cut the bottom batten to size and slot into the hem, stitch up the remaining side with ladder stitch.

19. Cut the rods 1cm (½in) shorter than the rod pockets and insert into each of the channels closest to the blind. Stitch either end of the rod pockets to close.

Rivets

20. Measure 5cm (2in) in from each side of the blind and mark the position of the rivet on the outer half of the rod pocket. Place two more marks at equal points along the rod pocket. Fold up the blind so that the sides are aligned and transfer the marks to the other rod pockets.

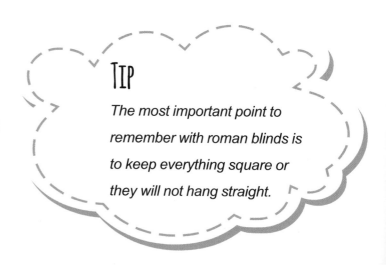

TIP

The most important point to remember with roman blinds is to keep everything square or they will not hang straight.

21. Punch a hole over each mark, place a rivet into the hole, place a flanged washer at the back and fix the rivet in place (Fig. 8).

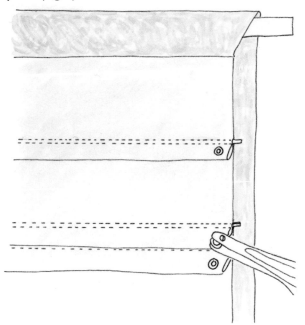

Fig. 8

Batten

22. Cut a wooden batten, 1cm (½in) shorter than the finished width of the blind. Drill three holes along the centre of the flat side. Position one just off centre by 2cm (¾in), and the other two, 7cm (2¾in) in from each end. (This is so that the fixing screws do not collide with the screw eyes that carry the cord.)

23. Cover the batten with lining fabric. Staple the fabric along one long edge, slightly stretching the fabric. Wrap the fabric around the batten and trim so that you have no more than 2cm (¾in) to turn under and staple in place. At each end trim to 5cm (2in) and cut away a wedge of fabric from the side with the staples, cut down at an angle to the end of the fabric, reducing the bulk of fabric. Make a neat parcel by wrapping the fabric around the end and staple on the flat side. Mark the fixing holes with the bradawl.

24. Staple the hook and loop fastening to the top of the batten, attach the blind and fold up the blind so that all of the rivets are lined up. Mark the position of the screw eyes on the narrow underside of the batten and fix the screw eyes in place (note that this is for a face fixing not a recess fixing). Position one extra screw eye 2cm (¾in) from the end of the batten to carry the cord to the end of the batten - this can be on the side of your choice.

Cording your blind

25. Begin cording on the side where you have put the extra screw eye. Thread the cord through the screw eye and then through the one at the top of the first row of rivets, then through all of the rivets on that side of the blind. Tie the cord to the lowest rivet with a slip knot. Bring the cord half way down the side of the blind and cut (Fig. 9).

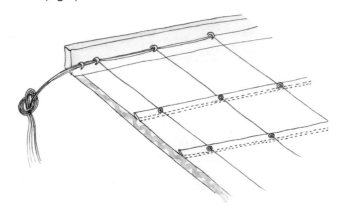

Fig. 9

26. Starting at the first screw eye for each cord, repeat with all the other rows of rivets (the last cord will travel across all of the screw eyes), cut the cord at the same length. After fixing the batten and hanging the blind, position a cleat on the window frame or wall and place an acorn at the end of the cords to tidy the ends.

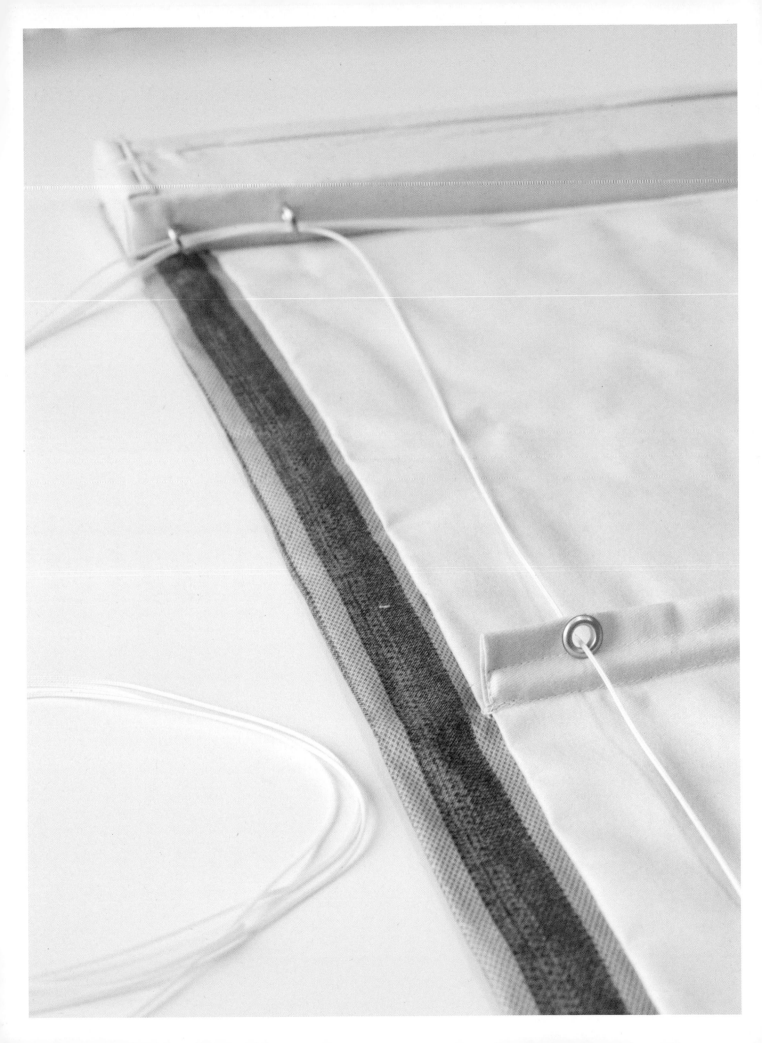

CHANGE YOUR STYLE!

Roman blinds can look so amazingly different with a change of fabric. These blinds are interlined to give added warmth and it also supports the fabric beautifully. Change the dimensions to fit your own windows; remember to add on 10cm (4in) for the side turnings and 14cm (5½in) for the hem and top turning, and don't forget to keep everything square!

Change Your Style using Tim Holtz Eclectic Elements, Ticking in Blue.

PATTERN GUIDE

Snuggly Pyjama Bottoms

Diagram A

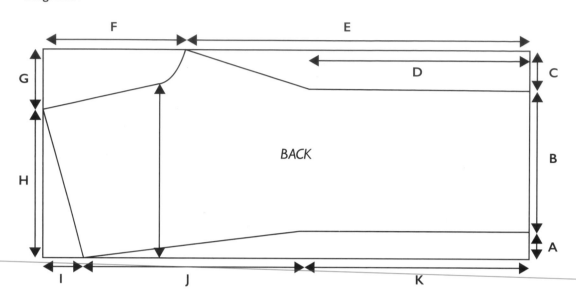

Back

Draw a rectangle 105 x 45cm (41⅓ x 17¾in) and then

draw out the pattern referring to Diagram A.

A = 5cm (2in)
B = 32cm (12¾in)
C = 8.5cm (3⅜in)
D = 48cm (19in)
E = 75cm (29½in)
F = 27.5cm (11in)
G = 12.5cm (4¾in)
H = 33cm (13in)
I = 8cm (3¼in)
J = 48.5cm (19in)
K = 48cm (18¾in)

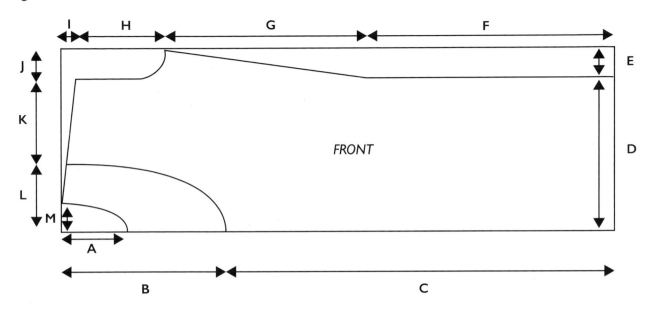

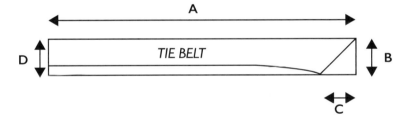

Front

Draw a rectangle 97 x 34cm (38 x 13½in)

and then draw the pattern, referring to Diagram B.

A = 16cm (6¼in)
B = 28.5cm (11¼in)
C = 70cm (27½in)
D = 27cm (10¾in)
E = 7cm (2¾in)
F = 48cm (18¾in)
G = 27cm (10¾in)
H = 19cm (7½in)
I = 3cm (1¼in)
J = 7cm (2¾in)
K = 21.5cm (8½in)
L = 10.5cm (4in)
M = 6cm (2½in)

Tie belt

Diagram C

Draw a rectangle, 65 x 8.5 cm (25½ x 3⅜in) and then

draw the pattern, referring to Diagram C.

A = 65cm (25½in)
B = 8.5cm (3⅜in)
C = 8.5cm (3⅜in)
D = 5.5cm (2¼in)

To enlarge or reduce the width of the pyjamas, calculate a quarter of the measurement that you wish to alter them by (for example if you want them to be 8cm/3in wider, a quarter is 2cm/¾in). Adjust the width of each pattern piece from a point vertical on the leg (for example reduce by 2cm/¾in on both front pieces and both back pieces).

ABOUT THE AUTHOR

Margaret Rowan has been designing and sewing all kinds of projects since childhood, creating many unusual and creative outfits as a teenager for herself and younger sisters!

This led her to a City and Guilds in Fashion and Textiles, and a degree from Camberwell School of Art and Craft in Textile Design and Printmaking.

Her love of making beautiful, functional projects has naturally taken her through a very interesting career, making and designing everything from wedding and ball gowns to soft furnishings for every kind of building - tiny cottages, stately homes and fabulous hotels.

As a passionate knitter she began working for Rowan Yarns in the mid 90s and this rekindled the workshop tutor inside her. After a year or two, she set up her own teaching studio and this led to writing her first book Stitch - The Complete Guide to Hand Sewing and Embellishing.

Teaching and encouraging other people to learn new skills is very important to her: "There is so much satisfaction in creating things for yourself, whatever form it takes. I hope this book will encourage and delight those who look inside and maybe take that first step in to the wonderful world of sewing!"

ACKNOWLEDGEMENTS

A huge thank you goes to four very talented and lovely ladies: Emily Davies, my lovely, patient Editor; Susan Campbell for your amazing illustrations; and Vicki Walker who made such a beautiful job of the projects in the alternative colourways.

Last, but not least, my Mum, who passed away in 2013, who encouraged me to sew and never once said: 'Are you really going out in that?!'

Thank you to Janome for their support and for their wonderful sewing machine, the Memory Craft 9800 QCP. Fantastic!!

Thank you also to Coats Crafts for supplying all the delicious fabric, Sharon Brant for asking me to work on the book, and to Honor Head for all her help, support and fabulous organization!

SUPPLIERS

Needcraft.co.uk
MD House
13 Abbey Mead Industrial Park
Brooker Road
Waltham Abbey
Essex EN9 1HU, UK
Tel: 01992 700311
www.needcraft.co.uk

Coats Crafts UK
Green Lane Mill
Holmfirth
West Yorkshire HD9 2DX, UK
Tel: 01484 681881
www.makeitcoats.co.uk

Merrick & Day
Redbourne Road
Redbourne
Gainsborough
Lincs. DN21 4TG, UK
Tel: 01652 648814
www.merrick-day.com

Stitch Craft Create
Brunel House,
Forde Close,
Newton Abbot,
Devon TQ12 4PU, UK
Tel: 0844 880 5852
www.stitchcraftcreate.co.uk

INDEX

A DAVID & CHARLES BOOK
© F&W Media International, Ltd 2014

David & Charles is an imprint of F&W Media International, Ltd
Brunel House, Forde Close, Newton Abbot, TQ12 4PU, UK

F&W Media International, Ltd is a subsidiary of F+W Media, Inc
10151 Carver Road, Suite #200, Blue Ash, OH 45242, USA

Text and Designs © F&W Media International, Ltd 2014
Layout and Photography © F&W Media International, Ltd 2014

First published in the UK and USA in 2014

Margaret Rowan has asserted her right to be identified as author of this
work in accordance with the Copyright, Designs and Patents Act, 1988.

The author and publisher have made every effort to ensure that all the
instructions in the book are accurate and safe, and therefore cannot accept
liability for any resulting injury, damage or loss to persons or property,
however it may arise.

Names of manufacturers and product ranges are provided for the
information of readers, with no intention to infringe copyright or
trademarks.

A catalogue record for this book is available from the British Library.

ISBN-13: 978-1-4463-0515-7 paperback
ISBN-10: 1-4463-0515-5 paperback

Printed in Italy by G. Canale & C.S.p.A. for:
F&W Media International, Ltd
Brunel House, Forde Close, Newton Abbot, TQ12 4PU, UK

10 9 8 7 6 5 4 3 2 1

Acquisitions Editor: Sarah Callard
Desk Editor: Honor Head
Project Editor: Emily Davies
Designer: Quail
Photographer: Jesse Wild
Illustrator: Susan Campbell
Senior Production Controller: Kelly Smith

F+W Media publishes high quality books on a wide range of subjects.
For more great book ideas visit: www.stitchcraftcreate.co.uk